BRITAIN IN OLD PHOTOGRAPHS

SHEFFIELD

GEOFFREY HOWSE

SUTTON PUBLISHING LIMITED

Sutton Publishing Limited
Phoenix Mill · Thrupp · Stroud
Gloucestershire · GL5 2BU

First published 1997

Title page: Paradise Street, *c.* 1910. Paradise Street and the adjacent Paradise Square consist of a series of Georgian town houses. Today the buildings are mostly used as offices. (SCL)

British Library Cataloguing in Publication Data
A catalogue record for this book is available from the British Library.

ISBN 0-7509-1419-X

Typeset in 10/12 Perpetua.
Typesetting and origination by
Sutton Publishing Limited.
Printed in Great Britain by
Ebenezer Baylis, Worcester.

The Church of St Peter and St Paul, Church Street, shortly before the First World War. It was built in about 1430, in the perpendicular Gothic style, on a site where Christian worship can be traced back over 1,200 years. It was raised to cathedral status in 1914. (SCL)

CONTENTS

Cathedral Church of St Peter and St Paul. The Shrewsbury Chapel, *c.* 1920. (SCL)

INTRODUCTION

Sheffield, with a population of over half a million, is England's fourth largest city and is built on seven hills and five river valleys. The rivers, which have played such an important part in the development of Sheffield, are the Don, Sheaf, Rivelin, Loxley and Porter. Sheffield is the greenest city in the country, as not only is there a wealth of parks in the city itself and woodland and open fields in the surrounding countryside, but a third of the land within Sheffield's boundaries lies within the Peak District National Park. The hills on which the city stands are covered in greenery and many streets are lined with trees. It is hardly surprising that when people visit Sheffield for the first time, many are shocked because they expect to see a lot of dust and grime, but what they find themselves visiting is a very attractive city indeed, one of the cleanest industrial cities in Europe.

Sheffield, which was granted a City Charter in 1893, has existed since before the Romans came to Britain. They built a road into Derbyshire and a fort at Wincobank. In 829 the Anglian Kings of Northumberland and Mercia met at Dore to settle their differences. The Normans built a castle, which stood on the site now occupied by Castle Market. That went the way of many castles during the period of the Civil War. By the middle of the eighteenth century Sheffield's population had grown to over 10,000 and, owing to the industrial expansion which took place there, had increased to an enormous 45,000 by 1800.

It was really the close proximity of plentiful supplies of water and the rich beds of iron ore that were responsible for the growth of the iron and steel industry in Sheffield. Early industry was quick to make use of the rivers as a source of power. Scores of dams were built in the river valleys, which held water to turn hundreds of water wheels. Timber was readily available and this was turned into charcoal for the smelting and forging industries. Coal provided energy during the Industrial Revolution but it was water power which made Sheffield famous for cutlery production. An early mention of the cutlery industry in Sheffield is in Geoffrey Chaucer's (*c.* 1340–1400) *Canterbury Tales*, when at the beginning of 'The Reeves Tale', Chaucer mentions 'A Sheffield thwitel [whittler] baar he in his hose', so it would appear that even in the fourteenth century Sheffield was noted for the industry in which it was to become, and remains to this day, the world leader.

From the earliest times the majority of metalworking was done by farmers from the nearby villages, who worked part-time, usually from home, and would rent time on one of the water-powered wheels or hammers. The hills in and around Sheffield made transportation of goods difficult, so specialised industries sprang up in areas where goods could be carried on a horse or on foot. The villages to the south of Sheffield, around Abbeydale and Norton, made scythes and sickles, whereas to the north in the historic village of Ecclesfield and Grenoside, nail and file making were the main industries. The cutlers worked principally in the town, along the banks of the River Don. The Cutlers' Company was set up in 1624 as a guild of craftsmen. By 1700 crude steel was being made in Sheffield, and in 1742 Benjamin Huntsman invented a way of melting blister steel in clay pots to make crucible steel, a high quality steel which remained the best steel available for over a hundred years. In 1858 Henry Bessemer brought his 'converter' to Sheffield. A crucible pot could only produce about 50 lb of steel in three and a half hours. This huge machine could produce 20 tons in just half an hour.

Expansion was rapid during the Industrial Revolution and in the closing years of the century the first factories were built, using steam engines to drive the machinery. By 1819 Sheffield Canal had opened and was used to bring in raw materials and to export finished goods. In 1837 the first railway appeared. The development of the railway industry meant more work for the people of Sheffield, because enormous quantities of high quality steel were needed. By the 1880s Sheffield was producing 'special steels' and development of the industry continued. In 1913 Harry Brearley of Sheffield discovered that by mixing chromium with steel the metal would not corrode. He had invented stainless steel. The iron and steel industry was at its height during the First World War; over 450,000 people lived in Sheffield at that time and over half the working population were engaged in the steel and cutlery producing industries. By 1970 40,000 people were working in these industries. By the mid-1980s the number had dropped to 12,000 and in 1997 there are about 8,000 engaged in steel and cutlery production. Surprisingly, more tons of steel are being produced in Sheffield than at any time during the industry's history. With the closure of so many factories engaged in the production of steel, the Sheffield landscape has changed dramatically. Many famous steel works closed and were demolished. Modern methods of production mean that only one man is needed where ten men were needed before. Today, not many Sheffield people make steel or cutlery, but Sheffield is still famous for it the world over.

Sheffield may have built its reputation on steel and cutlery, but it is not only industry for which it is justly famed. Sheffield is the birthplace of world soccer. Sheffield FC, the world's oldest football club, was founded in 1857. The first soccer rule book was produced in Sheffield, and forms the basis of the rules still in use today. Today Sheffield caters for all kinds of sport and has some of the finest sporting facilities anywhere in the country – so much so that in 1991 the World Student Games were staged there. It is also a city of learning. Sheffield boasts two universities, Sheffield University, which received its charter in 1905, and Hallam University, the former Sheffield City Polytechnic, opened in 1969 and granted university status in 1992.

In the photographs and illustrations in this book I have attempted to give the reader a glimpse of Sheffield's fascinating past. It has been impossible to include everything I would have liked and the choice of material has been purely personal. I have attempted to select material which has not appeared in other publications, but where certain subjects are concerned that has not been possible. I have not included some subjects because they have been given a great deal of exposure elsewhere. As we move towards the beginning of a new century I hope this book will serve as a reminder of the places and people of Sheffield's past.

Paradise Square, 1959. The square boasts Sheffield's finest surviving Georgian buildings. (SCL)

Cathedral Church of St Peter and St Paul. (SCL)

Tragedy on Broomhead Moors. Miss Norah Leary, aged 17, of Birch Road, Sheffield, died of exposure in the snow on Broomhead Moors. Her body was recovered from a snowdrift on 14 December 1937 and taken on a sledge to Broomhead Hall. The picture shows the rescue party in Mortimer Road, on its journey to Broomhead Hall. (Fox Photos Ltd, Manchester, SCL)

SECTION ONE

ROUND & ABOUT SHEFFIELD

The Corn Exchange, c. *1910. Built on the site of the old Shrewsbury Hospital in 1881 by the Duke of Norfolk, it was severely damaged by fire in 1947 and stood empty until it was demolished in 1964. (SCL)*

Abbeydale Industrial Hamlet, situated 4 miles from the city centre, between Beauchief and Dore, dates from the eighteenth century and contains workshops, warehouses and cottages. It has a rich industrial history and for the greater part of the nineteenth century was a major agricultural tool-producing complex. It is now a museum and has many interesting exhibits, such as a crucible furnace, a water-driven tilt forge and grinding wheel, as well as workshops displaying the numerous crafts associated with the hamlet's history. (SCL)

Workshops at Abbeydale Industrial Hamlet. (SCL)

Eighteenth-century cottages, situated in Priory Road, Ecclesfield. This photograph was taken by Cyril Slinn, shortly before they were demolished in 1972. (Cyril Slinn)

The Village Reading Room, Ecclesfield. Erected in 1722 on the site of an earlier wooden building, which had been used as a school (records show repairs to this school in 1573), this building served as a school until 1852 when it became a Mechanics Institute. It was used by various village organisations until its demolition in 1972. (Cyril Slinn)

Broom Hall stands in a leafy suburb at the junction of Park Lane and Broomhall Road. The suburb was created last century on part of the estate. Because of its historic associations, Broom Hall is one of Sheffield's most important houses. Part of the hall dates from 1500 and it has been owned by several prominent Sheffield families. Originally occupied by the powerful de Ecclesalls, it passed by marriage to the Wickersleys and then the Swyfts. In the eighteenth century it passed from the Jessop family to the Revd James Wilkinson, who was Vicar of Sheffield between 1754 and 1805. He was a colourful character and a magistrate who was noted for the harshness of his sentencing. In 1791 a mob gathered at Broom Hall and attempted to burn it down. Before any major damage could be done a company of dragoons arrived and dispersed the mob. One of the ringleaders was later hanged. Early in the nineteenth century Broom Hall was divided into three separate dwellings by the new owner, John Watson of Shirecliffe Hall. In 1829 he began granting building leases on the surrounding farmland. During the twentieth century Broom Hall gradually declined until there was a serious threat of demolition. Then, fortunately, the internationally famous designer David Mellor bought the hall, restored it and made it his home and base for cutlery manufacture. Broom Hall is presently divided into offices. This photograph, taken in 1989, shows part of the sixteenth-century hall. (SCL)

Broom Hall: the east wing, which was added in about 1790. (SCL)

The Mount, built between 1830 and 1832, was designed by Sheffield architect William Flockton to emulate a country house. It was in fact eight substantial houses set within a building of two-and-a-half storeys and seventeen bays long, the central pediment being supported by six Ionic columns. The pavilions are also supported by Ionic columns. It was nicknamed 'Flockton's Folly' because its situation overlooking Glossop Road at Broomhill was considered too far out of town to be of any interest to buyers, who would have needed substantial means to have been able to afford to reside in The Mount. However, it proved to be a popular place to live after all, and one of its first residents was the noted poet and hymn writer James Montgomery, who moved to The Mount in 1835 and died there in 1854. In the early 1940s the entire building was purchased by John Walsh Ltd, when their department store was destroyed in the Sheffield Blitz. In 1958 it was acquired by United Steels and it eventually became the regional headquarters of the British Steel Corporation. They sold it in 1978, and it is now divided into offices. The photograph shows The Mount during renovation in May 1959. (SCL)

Carbrook Hall is situated on Attercliffe Common. Once standing in isolated splendour, it is now surrounded by the extensive urbanisation which has completely transformed the Lower Don Valley over the last 150 years or so. In the late twelfth century the Blunts lived at Carbrook. Then, during the late Middle Ages a fine timber-framed house was erected and in 1623 a new stone wing was added. By this time a branch of the illustrious Bright family of Whirlow Hall occupied Carbrook Hall. John Bright of Carbrook, a Parliamentarian in the Civil War, was promoted to colonel in 1643 and made Governor of Sheffield Castle a year later. The hall was used by the Parliamentarians during the siege of Sheffield Castle in 1644. The Brights were an influential and extremely powerful Sheffield family, and today there are many reminders throughout Sheffield and district of the former residents of Carbrook Hall, including the district known as Brightside. On 26 February 1752 Mary Bright, daughter of Thomas Bright of Carbrook Hall, married Charles Watson Wentworth, 2nd Marquess of Rockingham, of Wentworth Woodhouse near Rotherham. The substantial fortune to which she was heiress made her a fitting match for Rockingham's high station. A much loved and respected Whig, Rockingham became prime minister twice and died in office in 1782. There were no children and Lord Rockingham's estates and the Bright legacy passed to his nephew, Earl Fitzwilliam. Mary, Marchioness of Rockingham, lived until December 1804. A descendant of the Brights, Admiral Southerton, sold the estate in 1819 and by 1855 Carbrook Hall had become a public house. The surrounding farmland was rapidly being developed into what was to become the heart of the world's premier steel-making centre. The timbered part of Carbrook Hall was demolished in about 1800. The remaining 1623 block is listed Grade II*. The hall has excellent moulded plaster ceilings and the upstairs parlour is an impressive panelled room with an extremely fine chimney-piece. The illustration is drawn and etched by E. Blore, and shows Carbrook Hall before the demolition of the timber portion. Carbrook Hall is still a public house. (SCL)

Carbrook Hall, *c.* 1900. (SCL)

Carbrook Hall: the upstairs parlour, and an excellent view of the panelling and chimney-piece. Note the superbly crafted plasterwork. (SCL)

Beauchief Hall was erected by Edward Pegge in 1671. The estate on which it was built was owned by the Strelley family from 1573. It passed through marriage in 1648 to the Pegges and, with a change of name to Pegge-Burnell, the family remained in residence until 1909, when William Wilson III, of Sharrow Mills snuff manufacturing family, purchased the hall and it became his family home. Since the 1950s the hall has been used for a variety of purposes: De La Salle College occupied it, then it became a hotel and latterly it has been used as corporate headquarters. The photograph shows a view of the hall from the south. It was taken from a lantern slide and shows the hall at the turn of the century. (SCL)

Beauchief Hall stables. This photograph was taken by Mr N.V. Bell in 1952. (SCL)

Cathedral Church of St Peter and St Paul: the extensions of 1940–50. (A.F. Kersting of London, SCL)

Cathedral Church of St Peter and St Paul, showing extensions, *c.* 1970. (J.A. Coulthard, Collegiate Crescent, Sheffield, SCL)

Church Street, Ecclesfield, *c.* 1910. (Cyril Slinn)

St Mary's Lane, Ecclesfield, *c.* 1875. This is a steep lane flanked by seventeenth-century cottages that connects Upper Ecclesfield with the village green and Lower Ecclesfield. (Cyril Slinn)

One of the earliest photographic images known to exist of Ecclesfield, this collotype shows St Mary's Church in about 1840. It shows the church before the enlargement of the churchyard and the building of the bier house in 1842. The original was found being used as a stiffening card behind another picture. (Cyril Slinn)

A view of St Mary's Church, Ecclesfield, *c.* 1960. St Mary's is one of the finest churches to be found anywhere in England. Known as 'the Minster of the Moors', it is largely perpendicular in style, although there are some earlier features. Its parish once covered 78 square miles. In the churchyard are buried the historian and antiquarian the Revd Joseph Hunter, and Alexander John Scott, Chaplain to Lord Nelson at the Battle of Trafalgar, who cradled the dying admiral in his arms. The celebrated Dr Gatty, who is the subject of a later photograph in this book, married Scott's daughter, Margaret, and on his death in 1903 was buried in the same vault as Scott. Dr Gatty was author of several books. His second daughter, Juliana Ewing, was a noted children's author. In one of her books, her invention of the Brownies inspired Baden-Powell to create a junior branch of the Girl Guides. (Cyril Slinn)

The Vicarage, Ecclesfield, 1966. This exceptionally fine vicarage was built in 1823. The nursery wing, which is the portion of the building jutting out from the back, was added to accommodate the Gatty children. Dr Gatty was Vicar of Ecclesfield from 1839 to 1903. He fathered ten children between 1840 and 1855. The Vicarage was demolished in 1966/67 and replaced by an extraordinary looking flat-roofed bungalow of modern design, totally at odds with the surrounding buildings. (Cyril Slinn)

A view of 'the Minster of the Moors' and Ecclesfield Vicarage, shortly before the Vicarage was demolished. (Cyril Slinn)

Part of the ring of eight bells from St Mary's Church, which were sent away for re-hanging in 1952. (Cyril Slinn)

Dr Gatty and his curate Mr Girling pictured on a lantern slide, unfortunately cracked in several places. Dr Gatty's *Life At One Living*, published in 1884, records life in the village of Ecclesfield during his incumbency. (Cyril Slinn)

The Jeffcock Memorial Fountain, Ecclesfield, was erected as a memorial to Thomas Jeffcock JP, DL, who died on 13 August 1900. He was a local benefactor. In the photograph are Mr Wass, with walking stick, Mr Dunstal, with bowler hat, and Florence Stringer. (Cyril Slinn)

Gatty Memorial Hall, Ecclesfield, was built in 1904 as a memorial to the late vicar, Dr Alfred Gatty, by public subscription. It is still used a parish room for meetings and social functions. (Cyril Slinn)

A view of Upper Ecclesfield, *c.* 1906. It shows the bolt and nail factory, the Independent Chapel (1819), the Methodist New Connection Chapel (1834) and the newly built Gatty Memorial Hall (1904). The Congregational Chapel (last building on the left) is now a private residence. (Cyril Slinn)

Stocks Hill, Ecclesfield, 1906. The building dominating the back centre of the photograph is the Feoffees Hall. A feoffee was a member of a board of trustees who administered land for charitable and public purposes. The history of the feoffees in Ecclesfield, of which there were originally fourteen, dates back to 1549. The hall seen here was built in the 1730s, and was demolished in 1968. In the photograph a group of children have been waylaid on their way home from school. In the group are Horace Hartley, with the basket, Florence Hemingfield and Mary Loxley, with the rolled-up pinafore in which she was carrying a cabbage, purchased on the way home. The old White Bear Inn can be seen behind the children on the right. (Cyril Slinn)

The 'new' White Bear Inn, Stocks Hill, Ecclesfield, being constructed in the early 1900s. The old White Bear Inn can be seen behind it. (Cyril Slinn)

Mill Road, Ecclesfield, *c.* 1921. The road was also known as Dog Leg Lane, because of its shape. The tall chimney (demolished 1924) formed part of the flour mill. (Cyril Slinn)

View of the Greyhound and the Ball Inn, Ecclesfield, *c.* 1963. The area in the foreground has been completely cleared of eighteenth- and nineteenth-century buildings. (Cyril Slinn)

Ecclesfield Cinema, *c.* 1925. Built in 1920, it seated 685 patrons in stalls and balcony. It opened on 1 June 1921 with the film *Broken Blossoms*, starring Lilian Gish. It closed during 1930, then re-opened with sound on 7 March 1932, with *King of Jazz*. It was purchased by Essoldo on 11 September 1950 and closed once and for all on 7 February 1959. The last film to be shown was *Young Lions*, starring Marlon Brando. (Cyril Slinn)

Ecclesfield Hospital Parade. The annual parade was a highlight in the life of the village and took place over the first weekend in July from 1891 to 1936. Decorated floats, mounted on horse-drawn carts and escorted by attendants in fancy dress wielding collecting tins, toured Sheffield on Saturday afternoon. This process was repeated on the Monday evening around the Chapeltown district. The floats consisted of a wooden framework covered in paper, carefully cut and trimmed and held together with a flour and water paste. The floats were made in great secrecy by different communities in the village, and hidden from the prying eyes of competing groups until the Saturday morning of the parade. After being assembled and judged the entire procession toured Sheffield. In this picture the community responsible for the windmill in the parade of 1907 pose by their float before moving off to the judging session. (Cyril Slinn)

Ecclesfield Hospital Parade: a decorated float depicting Rotherham parish church. (Cyril Slinn)

Another entry in the 1907 Ecclesfield Hospital Parade. Note the knee pads on the donkey. The groom is Mr Johnny Parkes. The owner of the cart, Mr Walter Stringer, leans on the cart. His daughter, Bonnie Stringer, and a friend, Miss Salt, are the passengers. Mrs Stringer and her mother in law, with Mrs Elliot, the aunt of Mrs Stringer senior, complete the picture. (Cyril Slinn)

Whit Monday, 1913. The scholars from Ecclesfield village Sunday Schools, preceded by their banners and the village band, march to Stocks Hill for hymn singing during the morning of Whit Monday. A tour of the village in the afternoon was followed by tea and games. (Cyril Slinn)

Hill Top, Yew Lane, Ecclesfield, 1906. The families occupying the cottages on the right pose for a photographer. Left to right: Mrs Hartley, carrying Annie, Mrs Susannah Whitham, carrying Connie. In the right background Mrs Stringer stands in the road and Mrs Janet Johnson stands on the pavement next to her. In the doorway is Mr Colin Witham, while standing next to him is Jack Witham, aged 3. He is crying because he wanted to go to the lavatory but had to wait until the photographer had finished. In the right foreground are Albert Beard and Ethel Green. The dog, Bellman, belonged to the Greens. (Cyril Slinn)

Hill Top, Yew Lane, Ecclesfield, 1972. Some of the cottages shown in the previous photograph have already disappeared. This photograph was taken shortly before the remaining cottages were demolished. (Cyril Slinn)

Customers of the Old Tankard Inn, Ecclesfield, preparing to leave on an outing. The bulk of the party travelled in a charabanc, as the next photograph shows. The landlord, Mr Moses Yeardley (in cap), and Mr W. Allen, local boot repairer (in high collar), pose before the motor car. Mrs Yeardley pretends to act as chauffeuse. (Cyril Slinn)

Customers of the Old Tankard Inn pose for a photograph before setting off on an outing. Mr Moses Yeardley stands to the left of the picture. (Cyril Slinn)

The Waggon and Horses, Burncross Road, Chapeltown, early 1900s. The site on which the buildings to the right stood is now occupied by a parade of shops, above which is the Asda supermarket. (John R. Wrigley)

The Pheasant Inn, Sheffield Lane Top, *c.* 1900. This public house marks the end of the climb up the hill from Ecclesfield, before the road descends to Firth Park and on past the Northern General Hospital. (SCL)

The George and Dragon, Beighton, *c.* 1900. Left to right: Mr Fitzaberley, Len Thompson senior, Mr Bartholomew, Frank Glover, who was killed in the First World War, and Mr Williamson. (Frank Money, SCL)

The Big Tree Hotel, Chesterfield Road, Woodseats, *c.* 1900. This eighteenth-century inn was formerly called the Masons Arms. A large horse chestnut tree stands in the forecourt, from which the public house took its name. (SCL)

The Big Tree, Woodseats, March 1991. This more recent building still has the big tree in its forecourt, but it is a sorry specimen compared with the tree in 1900. The big tree finally succumbed to the ravages of time in 1996 and it was replaced by a new tree, little larger than a sapling. It will be some considerable time before it reaches maturity. (SCL)

The Roebuck Tavern, Charles Street, 1965. (SCL)

The former Roebuck Tavern after refurbishment in 1994, renamed the Newt and Chambers, with an inn sign depicting a newt carrying a chamber pot. The name is a pun on the name of the world-famous former Sheffield firm of Newton Chambers, which had an extensive manufacturing complex in Chapeltown as well as an impressive sales office in the city. (SCL)

Fulwood Coffee House and Blacksmith's Arms, *c.* 1910. (R. Brown, SCL)

The former Fulwood Coffee House and Blacksmith's Arms, 1990s. It is now a private residence. (R. Brown, SCL)

Sheffield General Cemetery was built in 1836 at a cost of £13,000 on a 6-acre site. Such was its success that by 1848 a further 11 acres had been added, bringing the total cost to around £50,000. The cemetery was designed by the architect Samuel Worth. The gateway and screen and flanking walls were constructed by Worth in ashlar, in the Egyptian Revival style; the old chapel of 1836 has a Greek Doric portico, and the offices have Greek Doric columns. The new chapel, constructed by Worth in 1848, is like a church, with a west tower and spire by W. Flockton. A total of 77,837 people are known to have been buried here, in about 20,000 graves.

View from Sheffield General Cemetery towards St George's Church and Jessop's Hospital for Women, 1948. (SCL)

SECTION TWO

MARKETS, SHOPS & STORES

The unusual but imposing Austin Reed building in Fargate, c. 1950. It was formerly the trading premises of A.H. Holland Ltd. (SCL)

Fitzalan Market, *c.* 1845, from a lantern slide. (SCL)

Fitzalan Market Hall, 1895. The hall stood close to the present Fitzalan Square, and was demolished in 1930. This photograph originally appeared in R.S. Smith's *Old Sheffield*, vol. 4, p. 484. (SCL)

Cole Brothers was founded by three brothers in 1847. This building, which stood at the bottom of Fargate, was built in the 1860s. Cole's Corner was for a century a popular meeting place, as the illustration shows. (SCL)

Cole Brothers, Fargate, *c.* 1950. The premises were demolished after the department store moved to new premises in Barker's Pool in 1963. (SCL)

Cole Brothers' new store in Barker's Pool, September 1963. Cole Brothers is now a department store in the John Lewis Partnership. Barker's Pool dates back as far as 1435, when a Mr Barker built a reservoir, which existed until 1793. (SCL)

John Walsh established his store in 1896 in High Street. This photograph was taken in about 1905. The store was destroyed during the Sheffield Blitz in December 1940. Walsh's new store opened in 1953; in the 1970s it became Rackhams and is now House of Fraser. (SCL)

The Killing Shambles, Waingate, *c.* 1900. This was the slaughterhouse situated close to the city centre. Note the gulley in the middle of the cobbles, down which blood flowed. (SCL)

Castlefolds Market, January 1950. (SCL)

The Norfolk Market Hall opened in time for Christmas shopping in December 1851. Built on the site of the Tontine Hotel (1785–1849) at a cost of £40,000, it measured 296 ft × 115 ft × 45 ft high. Tyler & Co., Tobacconists, occupied the retail unit on the corner of Exchange Street. (SCL)

Norfolk Market Hall during the last weeks of trading, 1959. (SCL)

This dramatic photograph was taken by Charles Hall of Walkley Lane during the demolition of Norfolk Market Hall, November 1960. (SCL)

Castle Market, May 1995. This market, built on the site of Sheffield Castle, parts of which can still be seen beneath the market complex, was opened in 1963 on a site adjacent to the old Norfolk Market Hall. In addition to indoor stalls, selling everything from fine linens and fabrics to coal scuttles, there is also an impressive meat, fish and poultry market. (SCL)

The open Sheaf Market in 1967, which replaced the old Sheaf Market, popularly known as 'the Rag and Tag'. Behind can be seen Park Hill flats, a landmark in municipal housing when they were constructed in 1961. Together with high-rise flats on the adjacent Hyde Park site, the buildings were initially a source of great pride to Sheffield City Council. However, the concept of living in this style soon lost its appeal. All the high-rise flats, which rose to seventeen storeys, have been demolished. Some low-rise blocks were refurbished to create a Games Village for the World Student Games in 1991, but most have now disappeared from the Sheffield skyline. (SCL)

View of the indoor Sheaf Market from Exchange Place, 1995. The market has now been completely redeveloped and yet another new Sheaf Market has emerged. (SCL)

The premises of E.M. Taylor, butcher, Coleridge Place, Attercliffe, 1905. The boy standing on the doorstep is the young Colonel E.R. Bradley, Commanding Officer of the Local Defence Volunteers during the Second World War. (SCL)

Hovey's Shop, Angel Street, before December 1893 when the shop was destroyed by fire. This shop was the first in Sheffield to be illuminated by electricity, which was installed in 1881. The shop assistants slept above the premises and one of them was never found after the fire, which was described as one of the most dramatic of the period. (SCL)

The premises of John Bennett, butcher, taken prior to 1912. Road workers pose for a photograph. The road surface, made of compressed soil, was being replaced by asphalt. In spite of this the meat was still hanging in the open front of the shop. (Cyril Slinn)

The same butcher's shop as in the previous photograph, 19 November 1925. Meat still hangs in the open front of the shop, despite the shop now being on a bus route. (Cyril Slinn)

Ye Olde Sweete Shop, Woodseats, *c.* 1920. Mrs Pease stands on the doorsteps. Note the abundance of advertising signs. (SCL)

J. BEDFORD, PRACTICAL TAILOR, Church Street, ECCLESFIELD.

For well-made, smart, and stylish cut Garments, Ladies' and Gentlemen's.

We are also adding Youths' and Boys' Suits at most reasonable prices. Ladies' Coats and Skirts from 38/- Men's Suits from 34/- Overcoats from 28/- Made to your own measures. Boys' Sailor Suits from 2/11. Caps, Ties, Braces, Hunting Coats, Riding Breeches, Shooting, Cycling, and Golfing Suits, Coachmen's Livery

A continually-increasing turnover is proof that our Goods are more than holding their own. We shall spare no pains to give the best value. For whole families and repeat orders we quote cutting prices. Mourning Orders at a day's notice. First Class London Certificate for Cutting.

PLEASE NOTE. If you require a really good Boot or Shoe making to measure go to SMITH'S Post Office, ECCLESFIELD. SMITH'S can also supply you with ready made goods of the most up-to-date shapes and quality, at prices to suit all buyers.

Boot and Shoe Repairing a Speciality. A trial solicited. P.S.—Contractor to Wortley Union, Grenoside.

SMITH'S have got PICTURE POSTCARDS, and a variety of USEFUL & FANCY ARTICLES with Views of Ecclesfield on them—suitable for Presents.

Stationery, Fancy Goods, China, Glass, and Earthenware, Baskets, Brushes, Hearthrugs. Men's and Boys' Shirts, Fronts, Collars, Caps. Stockings, Wools, Worsteds, &c. All the leading Papers and Periodicals, &c., supplied to order.

PATENT MEDICINE VENDOR.

SMITH'S give you exceptional valve in all goods offered. Established over Quarter of a Century.

THOMAS DOVE,

Grenoside, nr. Sheffield.

Joiner, Wheelwright, & Undertaker.

Repairs promptly attended to.

DEALER IN ANTIQUE FURNITURE.

W. C. RIDGE,

Floodgate, ECCLESFIELD.

CARRIAGE PROPRIETOR, CARTING CONTRACTOR.

ESTIMATES FREE. Telephone: No. 19.

Telegrams: Ridge, Floodgate, Ecclesfield.

Established 1877.

COALS. COALS.

THOS. WM. MALLISON,

ECCLESFIELD.

Sole Agent for Wharncliffe, Silkstone, and Flockton Collieries. Prices on application for large or small quantities.

Coals or Gas Coke delivered in Ton or Bags.

Cash or Weekly Payments. Furniture Remover.

SAM. SORSBY,

CARRIER BETWEEN ECCLESFIELD, SHIREGREEN, & SHEFFIELD.

From Ecclesfield:—Tuesdays, Wednesdays, and Fridays at 12 a.m. Saturdays at 9-30 a.m.

From Sheffield:—"Bull and Mouth," Waingate, each day 5 p.m.

Coal Dealer and Carting Contractor.

Two pages of advertisements from Ecclesfield Parish Magazine, January 1903. (Cyril Slinn)

W. R. UNWIN,

ECCLESFIELD, Nr. SHEFFIELD.

MANUFACTURER OF . .

Head Stones, Monuments, Crosses, Ledger Tombs, Obelisks, and all kinds of Memorial Work in Stone or Marble.

Agent for some of the best firms in Scotch and other Granite.

Letters neatly cut in all Varieties, and Painted, Gilded, or filled in with Lead.

ELLIS'S,

St. Mary's Lane, Ecclesfield,

FOR

INCANDESCENT ACCESSORIES.

MANTLES—Welsbach, 6d.; Voelker, 4½d. each.
A Guarantee, 3½d. each.
For 1 dozen lots, less 6d. per dozen.

CHIMNEYS—6 in. straight, 2d. each; 8 in., 3d. each.
Domestic Jena, 5½d. each; Opal Jena, 7d. each.

Globes of various descriptions, all at reasonable prices. Complete light from 1s. 3d. each.
Pendants to order.

· Agent for Nelson's Widow Pension Tea.

G. CAMPLIN,

Moorside Terrace, . .
Ecclesfield Common.

Joiner, Wheelwright,
. and .
General Undertaker.

Coffins made on the shortest notice at reasonable prices.

REPAIRS TO PROPERTY, &c.

W. ALLEN,

St. Mary's Lane, ECCLESFIELD.

HAND-SEWN

Boot and Shoe Maker.

Repairs a Speciality.

Gent's Boots, Soled and Heeled		2s. 6d.
Ladies' „	„ „	1s. 6d.
Children's	„ „	1s. 0d.

Hand-sewn Boots made to measure from 14s. 6d.

Prudential Assurance Company.

INVESTED FUNDS £47,000,000.

Ordinary and Industrial Policies Issued.

AGENT—
FRANK BUTTON,
Yew Lane,
ECCLESFIELD.

F. B. will be glad to call and supply you with all information.

The *Telegraph and Star* offices, and John Atkinson's shop ('Fashions, Footwear and Fancies') complete with bunting and flags for VE Day, May 1945. (SCL)

SECTION THREE

TRANSPORT

Electric tram no. 248 at Fulwood Terminus, c. 1958. This tram was in service between 1936 and 1960. (SCL)

View of Sheffield Canal Basin, 1887. (F.W. Smith, Cockshutt Avenue, SCL)

Tinsley Locks, 1890. The imposing Old Toll House was demolished in about 1935. A pair of architecturally uninteresting semi-detached houses now provide accommodation for staff of the once busy Sheffield Ship Canal. (SCL)

Sheffield Midland Railway station, 1895. This view of the canopied entrance first appeared on a lantern slide. (SCL)

Train collision at Woodhouse Junction. (SCL)

Horse-drawn tram no. 9 on the Sheffield to Attercliffe and Tinsley Route, 1896. (SCL)

Horse-drawn tram no. 24 passing the Hillsbro' Inn, Proprietor and Licensee Henry Wilkinson, Hillsborough Corner, *c.* 1900. (SCL)

Chapeltown station, Great Central Railway, *c.* 1912. This station served the famous Newton Chambers works, which as well as producing high quality iron and steel products was responsible for major feats of international engineering. But perhaps the trade name for which Newton Chambers will always be remembered is Izal, the germicidal oil from which so many other products sprang. (John R. Wrigley, SCL)

Sheffield Midland Railway station, *c.* 1900. The principal edifice remains largely unchanged almost a hundred years later, but the landscape behind has changed dramatically. The innovative Park Hill flats have dominated the skyline immediately behind the Midland station for over three decades. With the demise of a considerable portion of that major building project, who can begin to guess what might appear on the rising land behind the station in years to come? (SCL)

Ecclesfield Midland Railway station, built 1898, *c.* 1905. (Cyril Slinn)

Tram no. 220, seen here on the Owlerton route, was in service between 1904 and 1938. The open top was covered in 1909. (SCL)

Sheffield to Lincoln train, 1908. Engine no. 437 was a 4–4–0 tender locomotive. (British Coal, SCL)

Sheffield Victoria station, *c.* 1905. (SCL)

Sheffield Midland Railway station, 1908: a clear view of engine no. 266. (SCL)

Attercliffe station on the Great Central line, looking south, 1916. The station closed on 26 September 1927. (SCL)

Midland Railway construction at Dore and Totley station, *c.* 1900. (SCL)

A similar view of Dore and Totley station, May 1968. (SCL)

Church Street, Ecclesfield, *c.* 1912. Note the recently metalled road. The early omnibus, known as Kitchener, makes its way from Chapeltown to Firth Park via Ecclesfield village. (Cyril Slinn)

Electric tram no. 252 was in service from 1905 to 1923. It is seen here in about 1910. (SCL)

A bus during the First World War, entering Collegiate Crescent. It is carrying Belgian casualties. (SCL)

The Crown and Globe Inn, Stannington, *c.* 1921/22. Left to right: Harry Thrale and Charles Holmes, standing in front of the Ford bus, Arthur Pickering, standing in front of the Traffic bus and Mr Billy Gillott leaning on the Guy bus. The three buses ran on the Stannington to Main Bridge route. (Mrs Holder, SCL)

Electric tram no. 182 on the Meadowhead route. This tram was in service from 1934 to 1957, and was photographed in January 1956. (SCL)

Sheffield Midland Railway station: the old waiting room on platform no. 1. (SCL)

Sheffield Victoria station, 1967. The most interesting aspect of this photograph is the notice board displaying the various prices of rail fares to London from four destinations, within less than a 25 mile radius. (SCL)

Darnall station, 1962. Mrs Lena Marsh and Mrs Kath Ledger keep up the good work to ensure that the station looks its best, as the winner of the Eastern Region Best Kept Station Award surely must. (Bernard Eyre, SCL)

Mr J. Brent (station master 1947–62), Mrs Kath Ledger and Mrs Lena Marsh pose for a photograph on the platform of Darnall station, summer 1962. (Bernard Eyre, SCL)

Electric tram no. 416, *c.* 1955. The tram was in service from 1919 to 1956. (SCL)

Electric tram no. 510 during Last Tram Week, 7 October 1960. (SCL)

Victoria station: closing day, 5 January 1970. (SCL)

Victoria station, 3 August 1981: shortly before demolition. (SCL)

Midland Railway station, 14 May 1965. (SCL)

Midland Railway station, after the façade was cleaned in August 1983. The high rise blocks of Hyde Park dominate the skyline. (SCL)

Norfolk Park?

View of Canal Wharf, from Hyde Park flats, *c.* 1970. (SCL)

Canal Basin, January 1989, before complete restoration and development. (SCL)

Canal Basin, March 1996, after restoration. (SCL)

Meadowhall Interchange, serving the Meadowhall Shopping Complex, August 1991. (SCL)

It's strange how things turn about face. The trams disappeared from Sheffield in 1960, and most people thought they would never be seen on the streets again. In May 1994 the new Super Tram took its first journey through the streets of Sheffield, and travelling by tram is now a very popular mode of transport once again. (SCL)

Section Four

Sports & Pastimes

Sheffield Wednesday FC, winners of the FA Cup in 1935. Captain Robert Starling carries the trophy. This photograph originally appeared in Football in Sheffield *(1962) by Percy Young. (SCL)*

Soccer was born in Sheffield. This photograph shows the Sheffield Football Team in April 1876. Sheffield FC, founded on 24 October 1857, is the world's oldest football club. Matches were first played between teams made up of club members. Sheffield FC now plays in local leagues. (SCL)

Sheffield United Football Club, 1890–1. Note the narrow stripes on the shirts. Three players are wearing the badge, and one the cap of Sheffield and Hallamshire FA. Back row, left to right: Harry Lilley, Mr Stokes, J.B. Wostinholm (Secretary), -?-, Mr Howlett, Mr Witham, Mr Houseley (trainer). Centre: -?-, -?-, -?-, Mr Howell, -?-, H.H. Stones (Assistant Secretary). Front: -?-, -?-, Mr Watson, -?-. I am grateful to Mr D.K. Clarebrough for the information supplied about Sheffield United FC. (SCL)

Sheffield United Football Club Cup Final team, 1901. Standing, left to right: Hedley, Morren, Johnson, Thickett, Field, Boyle, Priest, Needham. Seated: Bennett, Foulke, Beer, Lipsham (reserve). I am grateful to Mr D.K. Clarebrough for supplying the names of the players. (SCL)

Sheffield Wednesday Football Club, League Champions, 1902–3. (SCL)

Burgoyne Road School Football Team, 1907. This team won the Clegg Football Shield, and each player wears a silver medal. Headmaster, Frank Gray, stands on the right. He later moved to Greaves Street School. Other masters are Mr Tyas (Greenhow Street), sitting right, Mr Williamson, standing left, and Mr Bott, sitting left. The Captain, Master Bagshawe, is at the front on the left. Also in the photograph are Billy Osborne, Billy Kay, Billy Hall, Revill Marshall, Master Deakin and Master Haray. (Miss Bagshawe, SCL)

Edgar Allen FC, 1920: winners of the first ever Tinsley Charity Cup. Amongst those in the photograph are J. Scrivens, H. Pinchers, J. Bigadyke, F. Hammond, L. Glover, Mr Senior, Mr Richards (extreme right, Director of Edgar Allen). (SCL)

Darnall Wesleyan Football Team, 1923/4. Back row, left to right: Rackham, Coombes, George, George Turner, Bob Wilson, John Lawrence, Walker. Third row, standing: all unknown. Second row, seated: Wainwright, -?-, Frank Rackhams. Front row: Percy Rhodes, -?-, George Booth, Wainwright, -?-. (SCL)

Newhall Boys School Football Team, *c.* 1928. The girl at the centre in the front was the bookmaker's daughter, who was known as 'Girlie'. She is in the photograph because her father bought the football kit for the entire team. (SCL)

Sheffield Wednesday FC, League Champions 1928/9. (SCL)

Sheffield Wednesday FC, winners of the FA Cup in 1935. In the photograph are the players, officials and directors of the club. Back row, left to right: Tommy Walker, -?-, -?-, Jack Surtees, Sam Powell (trainer), Wilf Sharp, Jack Palethorpe, -?-, Jackie Robinson. Third row: Eric W. Taylor, Ellis Rimmer, Les Fenwick, Jack Brown, Ronnie Starling, Joe Nibloe, Ted Catlin, Walt Millership, George Irwin (trainer), George Ainsley, Horace Burrows, W.H. Walker (secretary/manager). Second row: W.F. Wardley, E.G. Flint, S.H. Nixon, P. Bowker, W.G. Turner, Sir Charles Clegg, W. Fearnehough, A.J. Blanchard, E. Mills, Dr Ian Rhind, J. Swallow. Front row: Mark Hooper, -?-, Sedley Cooper, Harry Grange, George Drury, Jack Thompson. (SCL)

FA Cup semi-final, 3 April 1993, Sheffield United vs Sheffield Wednesday. The match was played at Wembley. (SCL)

FA Cup semi-final, Wembley, 3 April 1993. The final score. (SCL)

Darnall Cricket Ground, 1824, engraved by Robert Isaac Cruikshank (1789–1856). The cricket ground shown was the second at Darnall. The first opened in 1821, but the following year the stand collapsed and two spectators were killed. The owner, a Mr Steer, immediately set about building a larger ground nearby. It was ready for play in 1824, and provided seating for 8,000 spectators on artificial terraces. In spite of the high quality of the ground, Darnall was 3 miles from the centre of Sheffield, and the Hyde Park Ground just half the distance. Largely because of this, Hyde Park became the centre of Sheffield and Yorkshire cricket, and no cricket matches of any significance were played at Darnall after 1829. (SCL)

Bramall Lane Cricket Ground, 1885. (SCL)

Yorkshire vs Surrey at Sheffield, 14–16 June 1875. The Yorkshire team are as follows. Standing, left to right: G. Martin (Umpire), J. Thewlis, G. Pinder, G. Wyett, T. Armitage, J. Rowbotham, A. Hill and A. Greenwood. Seated: T. Emmett, J. Hicks, E. Lockwood and C.E. Ullathorne. (SCL)

Low Bradfield Cricket Team, *c.* 1910. Back row, left to right: PC Bowden, Robert Fretwell, Alwyn Harper, Sam Woodhouse, Spencer Elliott, Mr Darby. Second row: Mark Elliott, -?-, -?-, -?-, Horace Fretwell. Front row: -?-, -?-. (SCL)

Sheffield United Cricket XI, 1913. Standing, left to right: N. Atkin of Atkin Bros (Truro Works) lost a leg in the First World War; C.E. Nornable played for Derbyshire; J.N. Fraser was a director of Mappin & Webb; G.A. Buckley, a schoolmaster who played for Derbyshire, became headmaster of Duchess Road School; J. Robinson was an insurance agent; B. Wilkinson played for Yorkshire XI at cricket and for Sheffield United and England at football; son of a schoolmaster from Thorpe Hesley near Rotherham, he changed his name from Pickles to Wilkinson; J. Parkin played for Yorkshire XI as wicketkeeper, and was a native of Rotherham. Seated: E. Needham, born in Chesterfield, played for Derbyshire at cricket, Sheffield United at football and was captain of England, and was known as 'Nudger' Needham, the 'prince' of halfbacks; Jeffcock of Handsworth Hall, G.N. Dodworth (Captain), a Sheffield solicitor and a major in the TA; G. Weller, played for Yorkshire at cricket and Sheffield Wednesday at football; he later became a trainer for Sheffield United FC; J.E. Elms, born at Pitsmoor, played for Yorkshire at cricket and was a champion carnation grower. I am most grateful to Mr Gordon Nornable for supplying the information about his father, Ernest Nornable, mentioned above, and about other members of Sheffield United Cricket XI. (SCL)

Sheffield United Cricket Club, 1949. Back row, left to right: R. Hall, C. Lee, E. Burgin, J. Ashman, D. Lane, F. Melluig, Mr Burgin (scorer). Front row: L. Morgan, C. Turner, K. Lee, R. Douglas and H. Parkin. (SCL)

Cricket match at Bramall Lane ground, *c.* 1959. This view looks towards the south-east stands and pavilion. (SCL)

Beighton Miners' Welfare Bowling Club, 1928. (Frank Money, SCL)

Bowling green at the Old Pheasant Inn, Carbrook. William Salt is in the straw boater, on the right. (Mr E.M. Gunn, SCL)

Customers of Ye Old Tankard Inn, Ecclesfield, out fishing. The match was held at Ely on 27 July 1911. (Cyril Slinn)

Ecclesfield Rifle Club held their meeting in a quarry in the village. The members of the club were known jocularly as the 'Butterfly Shooters', as they rarely hit the target. Back row, left to right: J.H. Butterworth, Moses Yeardley, W. Hinchcliffe, W. Unwin, W.H. Marshall, W. Green, F. Gregory, I. Copley. Front row: J.W. Granger, Mr Kirk, Miss Kirk, F. Robinson. Romance flourished in spite of the martial atmosphere: Miss Kirk became Mrs Copley. (Cyril Slinn)

Stag shoot on the Wharncliffe estate, between 1890 and 1898. The stag was for the Cutlers' Feast. On the right is William Laycock, headkeeper; on the left is James Lane. Frank Clarke is sitting on the cart. (SCL)

Section Five

Sheffield at Work

St Philip's churchyard, Infirmary Road. Behind is the famous Globe Works, the scene of several nineteenth-century trades union outrages. The musical play The Stirrings in Sheffield, *originally produced at Sheffield Playhouse in 1966, gives an excellent account of this troublesome period in Sheffield. (SCL)*

Jack Carl drystone grinding at J. Elliot and Sons, cutlers, Sylvester Street, 1981. (SCL)

J. Elliot and Sons: Mrs Gill is operating the pulling on machine. (SCL)

Pocket knife manufacture, April 1957. After over five years of research and testing at Joseph Rodgers and Sons Ltd, Pond Hill, a new hot-bonding process for the manufacture of pocket knives was developed. The method ensures complete rigidity of the blade without the need for through-riveted bolsters. In this photograph a small batch of knife blades is removed from the gas oven, in which they have been 'cured', a process which ensures complete adhesion of the parts. (Central Office of Information, Crown Copyright, SCL)

Joseph Rodgers and Sons Ltd, April 1957. Here pen-knives are being packed for export. Note the firm's distinctive trade mark, which was granted in 1682. (Central Office of Information, Crown Copyright, SCL)

Joseph Rodgers and Sons Ltd, 1957. Here Mr Bob Willerton, an employee for thirty years, works in the Forging Shop. He is stamping out a blade under the power hammer. (Central Office of Information, Crown Copyright, SCL)

Joseph Rodgers and Sons Ltd, 1957. After forging, hardening and tempering, knife blades are put through a series of polishing processes. The first of these, 'horsing', is being carried out by an operator sitting astride the horse, grinding a stainless steel blade. (Central Office of Information, Crown Copyright, SCL)

Knife grinding. This photograph, taken at F.A. Kirk (Cutlers) Ltd, in March 1957, shows an operator grinding down knife blades on a semi-automatic machine of British manufacture. (Central Office of Information, Crown Copyright, SCL)

Etching on knife blades at F.A. Kirk (Cutlers) Ltd, 1957. Here an operator is etching the words 'Sheffield Cutlery' on to fifteen knife blades simultaneously, by using a British-made Taylor–Hobson multiple etching machine. (Central Office of Information, Crown Copyright, SCL)

Above: Smoothing the surface of a knife after rough grinding at F.A. Kirk (Cutlers) Ltd, 1957. The operator is removing a blade from the semi-automatic double-heading machine. (Central Office of Information, Crown Copyright, SCL)

Left: Stamping out silver plate fish knives at Walker and Hall Ltd, March 1957. Sheets of nickel silver are being put through the stamping machine. (Central Office of Information, Crown Copyright, SCL)

At Walker and Hall Ltd an operator removes a batch of spoons from the plating vat, part of the scientifically controlled processing, March 1957. (Central Office of Information, Crown Copyright, SCL)

Fork filing at Lewis, Rose and Company Ltd, March 1957. The prongs of the forks on the table are joined by a narrow strip of metal. This is filed off before the final grinding and polishing process. Here an operator files the prong tips of New English style forks. (Central Office of Information, Crown Copyright, SCL)

Gimlet making in Ecclesfield. Mr John Thomas Ridge retired at the age of 90; his retirement and the closure of his smithy in 1969 severed a link with the metal working industries of the village, which had existed for over 800 years. (Cyril Slinn)

Section Six

Sheffield at War

Sheffield in flames, 15 December 1940. Sheffield was blitzed by the Luftwaffe on 12–13 and 15–16 December. (Mrs Hatfield, SCL)

Wedding of Emma Salt and Benny Twigg, during the First World War. Benny Twigg was in the Battle of the Somme, 1 July 1916: no trace of him was ever found. (Mrs E.M. Gunn, SCL)

War Bonds on sale during the First World War from a tank in Fitzalan Square. (Mrs D.M. Smith, SCL)

The Royal Army Medical Corps parade in West Street, 1914. (SCL)

Sheffield City Battalion during the First World War. (SCL)

Walter Appleyard JP, Lord Mayor of Sheffield, with Lt. Gen. Smuts and Admiral Sir John Jellicoe, during their visit to Sheffield, 1917. (SCL)

Peace celebrations in Stocksbridge. (SCL)

High Street in flames, 12 December 1940. (SCL)

Houses in all parts of Woodseats were badly damaged or destroyed on 12 December 1940. This one stood on Bocking Lane. (SCL)

Damage at the Jessop Hospital for Women, 12 December 1940. (SCL)

Damage to the Empire Theatre and shop property at the junction of Charles Street and Union Street, 12 December 1940. (SCL)

Severe damage was inflicted on St James Street, 13 December 1940. (SCL)

The LNER Goods Office, Stevenson Road, 15 December 1940. (SCL)

The Firth family installing their Anderson shelter at 33 Firbeck Road, Woodseats. The photograph was taken on 4 September 1940. The first air raid warning actually came during the night of 3/4 September, which encouraged the family to complete work on the shelter. Mrs Firth stands in the foreground, while Mr Firth is assisted by his 12-year-old daughter June Mary Firth. (Sheffield Archive, SCL)

WVS mobile canteen in St Mary's Road, December 1940. The canteen is a converted Rolls-Royce. (SCL)

Members of the Central Library staff in the kitchen preparing food for the homeless after the air raids in December 1940. Left to right: Miss J.W. Clare, Miss L. Relph, Miss K.M. Dawes, Miss J.W. Woodward, Miss E.H. Godfrey, and a voluntary helper. (SCL)

Members of the Central Library on the library roof for ARP training, 1940. Miss Lee of Woodseats is on the left of the second row; Miss M. Walton and Miss P. Charlesworth are on the right of the back row. (SCL)

York and Lancaster Regiment Home Guard, Wardlow, *c.* 1944. Col. W. Howson O/C 69th Battalion, Col. Cheltenham, Maj. E.R. Bradley O/C 'E' Corp 69th Battalion, Col. E. Barnsley O/C Sheffield Cadet Corps, Col. Kemp, Col. Wardlow, Maj. Johnson. (SCL)

Officers of the 67th (Sheffield) Battalion, West Riding Home Guard, July 1944. (SCL)

AA gun emplacement, Warminster Road, Second World War. (SCL)

Crowds gather to watch as a RAF barrage balloon is inflated on Crookesmoor Recreation Ground, *c.* 1940. (SCL)

D-Day street party on Rotherham Street, Attercliffe. (SCL)

VE-Day celebrations, 8 May 1945. A flag is raised by boys and girls in Rushdale Square, as they prepare to light a bonfire and burn the effigy of Hitler during part of their celebrations. (SCL)

SECTION SEVEN

ROYAL VISITS

Visit of His Majesty King Edward VII and Her Majesty Queen Alexandra to the River Don Works of Vickers Sons and Maxims Ltd, 12 July 1905. (SCL)

Victoria station decorated for HRH Prince of Wales' visit, 1875. (SCL)

The Pinstone Street arch created to form part of the lavish decorations for Her Majesty Queen Victoria's visit to Sheffield in 1897. (SCL)

Her Majesty Queen Victoria's carriage approaches the steps of Sheffield's new Town Hall, 1897. (SCL)

His Majesty King Edward VII and Her Majesty Queen Alexandra at the opening of Sheffield University, 12 July 1905. (SCL)

Decorations for the Royal visit, July 1905. (SCL)

Weston Park decorations for the Royal visit, July 1905. (SCL)

Decorations in Fitzwilliam Street for the Royal visit, July 1905. (SCL)

Tram no. 167 decorated for the Royal visit, July 1905. (SCL)

Electric tram decorated for the coronation of His Majesty King George V, 1911. (SCL)

Another electric tram similarly decked out to celebrate the coronation, 1911. (SCL)

SECTION EIGHT

SHEFFIELD THEATRES

The Lyceum Theatre, December 1990. This view shows the refurbished proscenium arch and the impressive new safety curtain. (SCL)

The Alexandra Theatre and Opera House, seen here in about 1900, was built in 1836. Originally called the Adelphi, it was renamed the Alexandra Music Hall in 1865, when Thomas Youdan, who had previously owned the theatre, acquired it once again after his theatre and circus in Blonk Street was destroyed by fire. This much-loved theatre, popularly known as 'Tommy's' from 1865, was situated at the junction of the rivers Sheaf and Don in Blonk Street. The stage, reputed to be the largest in the provinces, was actually built over the River Sheaf. Even after the name change to the Alexandra Theatre and Opera House, the theatre was still 'Tommy's' to many Sheffield people, although during the theatre's latter years it was referred to as the 'Old Alec'. Because of the large stage, touring opera companies played there and productions of every type were performed, including the annual pantomime, which ran for three months every year from Christmas. There was great rivalry between this theatre and the Theatre Royal, but in general the two theatres complemented each other, the Alec providing a bill of family entertainment, the Theatre Royal concentrating on more serious fare. In 1914 Sheffield Corporation bought the theatre and demolished it in order to carry out a street improvement programme, which involved the widening of the road in Exchange Street. (SCL)

The Music Hall, Surrey Street, opened in 1823, was a deceptively large building. Just one room in this theatre could accommodate 1,000 patrons. It was photographed by W.H. Babington in about 1900. (SCL)

The Empire Theatre, known also as the Empire Music Hall and the Empire Palace, was situated in Charles Street. This theatre was built by Britain's most prolific and arguably finest theatre architect, Frank Matcham (1854–1920). The theatre opened in 1895 and during its glorious existence presented many of the greatest names in music hall, variety and musical comedy. Its loss to Sheffield and also the loss of its rival, the Hippodrome Theatre (1907–63), built by Bertie Crewe, which stood on the site now occupied by the Grosvenor House Hotel, leaves a gaping hole, which can never be filled, for we will never see the like of these magnificent theatres again. The Empire closed in May 1959. This photograph, taken in 1959, shows the Empire shortly before demolition. (SCL)

Frank Matcham's magnificent auditorium at the Empire Theatre. (SCL)

Demolition of the Empire Theatre, 1959. (Mr W.H. Cole, SCL)

A last view of the Empire Theatre's proscenium arch during demolition, with the safety curtain lowered. (Mr W.H. Cole, SCL)

View of the Lyceum Theatre and Theatre Royal, *c.* 1900. The Lyceum was built on the site of the City Theatre and Circus, which closed after a disastrous fire in 1893. The new theatre was built by the distinguished architect W.G.R. Sprague (1865–1933), who was responsible for creating some of the most beautiful theatres in London. The Lyceum is his only remaining theatre in the provinces. It opened in October 1897, when, after the National Anthem had been sung, the audience sat down to watch a performance of *Carmen* by the Carl Rosa Opera Company. The Theatre Royal (1773–1935) was altered several times, having being almost completely rebuilt in 1855. Frank Matcham also made various alterations to the theatre in 1901. It was almost completely destroyed by fire during the pantomime season in December 1935. (SCL)

Disaster struck at the Theatre Royal on the night of 30 December 1935. (SCL)

Firemen try in vain to save Sheffield's much-loved Theatre Royal. (SCL)

The Theatre Royal after the disastrous fire. It was too badly damaged to be saved and the entire structure was demolished. (SCL)

The Lyceum Theatre, May 1989. Here the old fly tower and dressing room block are torn down. (SCL)

The Lyceum Theatre, May 1989: the auditorium before refurbishment. (SCL)

The Lyceum Theatre, December 1990. The new fly tower and dressing room block can be seen to the left. (SCL)

The Lyceum Theatre's newly refurbished auditorium, December 1990. (SCL)

View of the Crucible Theatre, Lyceum Theatre and Odeon, 7 March 1992. (SCL)

ACKNOWLEDGEMENTS

I am most grateful for the assistance I have been given during the compilation of this book. I would like to thank my Personal Assistant John D. Murray, Mr Cliff and Mrs Margaret Willoughby, Mr Herbert and Mrs Doreen Howse, Mr David and Mrs Christine Walker, of Walkers Newsagents, Hoyland, Mr Darren J. Walker, Mr Simon Edwards, Mr Cyril Slinn, for allowing me access to his collection and for the detailed information he provided me with, Mr Doug Hindmarch, senior Local Studies Librarian, Sheffield Central Library and the library staff, Miss Tracy P. Deller, Miss Iris Deller, the late Mr Terry Murray (1951–97), the late Mr George Thomas Hayes (1916–97), Mrs Doris Hayes, Mr David G.T. Hayes, Mr Nicholas M. Hayes, Mr James Friend, Mr Frank Hully of Ecclesfield, Mr Paul T. Langley Welch, Mr Frank Money, Mr J.A. Coulthard, the late Mr W.H. Cole (1903–96), Mr David H. Cole, Mr Gordon Nornable, Mr Bernard Eyre, Mr N.V. Bell, Mrs Jean Phillips, Mr Jonathan Crabb of the Central Office of Information, Mr John R. Wrigley, Mr Denis Clarebrough, Mrs E.M. Gunn, June M. Firth, Mrs D.M. Smith, W.H. Babington, Mr R.S. Smith, R. Brown, Mr Percy Young, A.F. Kersting, Mr Charles Hall, Mr Raymond Sargent, Miss Bagshawe, Vince Linnane, Jeremy Hale, Sean Lambe, Harry Grounds of Class Method Ltd, Mrs Cartlige, Richard Huggett, Ricki S. Deller, Joanna C. Murray Deller, Joanna Pyke, Anne Bennett, Simon Fletcher and Annabel Fearnley.

BRITAIN IN OLD PHOTOGRAPHS

ɔerystwyth & North Ceredigion
·ound Abingdon
:ton
derney: A Second Selection
ong the Avon from Stratford to
Tewkesbury
trincham
nersham
·ound Amesbury
ıglesey
·nold & Bestwood
·nold & Bestwood: A Second
Selection
·undel & the Arun Valley
shbourne
·ound Ashby-de-la-Zouch
ro Aircraft
lesbury
lham & Tooting
nburyshire
rnes, Mortlake & Sheen
rnsley
th
aconsfield
dford
dfordshire at Work
dworth
verley
xley
deford
lston
rmingham Railways
shop's Stortford &
Sawbridgeworth
shopstone & Seaford
shopstone & Seaford: A Second
Selection
ack Country Aviation
ack Country Railways
ack Country Road Transport
ackburn
ackpool
·ound Blandford Forum
etchley
ɔlton
ɔurnemouth
·adford
·aintree & Bocking at Work
·econ
·entwood
·idgwater & the River Parrett
·idlington
·idport & the Bride Valley
·ierley Hill
·ighton & Hove
·ighton & Hove: A Second
Selection
·istol
·ound Bristol
·ixton & Norwood
ırly Broadstairs & St Peters
·omley, Keston & Hayes

Buckingham & District
Burford
Bury
Bushbury
Camberwell
Cambridge
Cannock Yesterday & Today
Canterbury: A Second Selection
Castle Combe to Malmesbury
Chadwell Heath
Chard & Ilminster
Chatham Dockyard
Chatham & Gillingham
Cheadle
Cheam & Belmont
Chelmsford
Cheltenham: A Second Selection
Cheltenham at War
Cheltenham in the 1950s
Chepstow & the River Wye
Chesham Yesterday & Today
Cheshire Railways
Chester
Chippenham & Lacock
Chiswick
Chorley & District
Cirencester
Around Cirencester
Clacton-on-Sea
Around Clitheroe
Clwyd Railways
Clydesdale
Colchester
Colchester 1940–70
Colyton & Seaton
The Cornish Coast
Corsham & Box
The North Cotswolds
Coventry: A Second Selection
Around Coventry
Cowes & East Cowes
Crawley New Town
Around Crawley
Crewkerne & the Ham Stone
Villages
Cromer
Croydon
Crystal Palace, Penge & Anerley
Darlington
Darlington: A Second Selection
Dawlish & Teignmouth
Deal
Derby
Around Devizes
Devon Aerodromes
East Devon at War
Around Didcot & the Hagbournes
Dorchester
Douglas
Dumfries
Dundee at Work
Durham People

Durham at Work
Ealing & Northfields
East Grinstead
East Ham
Eastbourne
Elgin
Eltham
Ely
Enfield
Around Epsom
Esher
Evesham to Bredon
Exeter
Exmouth & Budleigh Salterton
Fairey Aircraft
Falmouth
Farnborough
Farnham: A Second Selection
Fleetwood
Folkestone: A Second Selection
Folkestone: A Third Selection
The Forest of Dean
Frome
Fulham
Galashiels
Garsington
Around Garstang
Around Gillingham
Gloucester
Gloucester: from the Walwin
Collection
North Gloucestershire at War
South Gloucestershire at War
Gosport
Goudhurst to Tenterden
Grantham
Gravesend
Around Gravesham
Around Grays
Great Yarmouth
Great Yarmouth: A Second
Selection
Greenwich & Woolwich
Grimsby
Around Grimsby
Grimsby Docks
Gwynedd Railways
Hackney: A Second Selection
Hackney: A Third Selection
From Haldon to Mid-Dartmoor
Hammersmith & Shepherds Bush
Hampstead to Primrose Hill
Harrow & Pinner
Hastings
Hastings: A Second Selection
Haverfordwest
Hayes & West Drayton
Around Haywards Heath
Around Heathfield
Around Heathfield: A Second
Selection
Around Helston

Around Henley-on-Thames
Herefordshire
Herne Bay
Heywood
The High Weald
The High Weald: A Second
Selection
Around Highworth
Around Highworth & Faringdon
Hitchin
Holderness
Honiton & the Otter Valley
Horsham & District
Houghton-le-Spring &
Hetton-le-Hole
Houghton-le-Spring & Hetton-le-
Hole: A Second Selection
Huddersfield: A Second Selection
Huddersfield: A Third Selection
Ilford
Ilfracombe
Ipswich: A Second Selection
Islington
Jersey: A Third Selection
Kendal
Kensington & Chelsea
East Kent at War
Keswick & the Central Lakes
Around Keynsham & Saltford
The Changing Face of Keynsham
Kingsbridge
Kingston
Kinver
Kirkby & District
Kirkby Lonsdale
Around Kirkham
Knowle & Dorridge
The Lake Counties at Work
Lancashire
The Lancashire Coast
Lancashire North of the Sands
Lancashire Railways
East Lancashire at War
Around Lancaster
Lancing & Sompting
Around Leamington Spa
Around Leamington Spa:
A Second Selection
Leeds in the News
Leeds Road & Rail
Around Leek
Leicester
The Changing Face of Leicester
Leicester at Work
Leicestershire People
Around Leighton Buzzard &
Linslade
Letchworth
Lewes
Lewisham & Deptford:
A Second Selection
Lichfield

Lincoln
Lincoln Cathedral
The Lincolnshire Coast
Liverpool
Around Llandudno
Around Lochaber
Theatrical London
Around Louth
The Lower Fal Estuary
Lowestoft
Luton
Lympne Airfield
Lytham St Annes
Maidenhead
Around Maidenhead
Around Malvern
Manchester
Manchester Road & Rail
Mansfield
Marlborough: A Second Selection
Marylebone & Paddington
Around Matlock
Melton Mowbray
Around Melksham
The Mendips
Merton & Morden
Middlesbrough
Midsomer Norton & Radstock
Around Mildenhall
Milton Keynes
Minehead
Monmouth & the River Wye
The Nadder Valley
Newark
Around Newark
Newbury
Newport, Isle of Wight
The Norfolk Broads
Norfolk at War
North Fylde
North Lambeth
North Walsham & District
Northallerton
Northampton
Around Norwich
Nottingham 1944–74
The Changing Face of Nottingham
Victorian Nottingham
Nottingham Yesterday & Today
Nuneaton
Around Oakham
Ormskirk & District
Otley & District
Oxford: The University
Oxford Yesterday & Today
Oxfordshire Railways: A Second Selection
Oxfordshire at School
Around Padstow
Pattingham & Wombourne
Penwith
Penzance & Newlyn
Around Pershore
Around Plymouth
Poole
Portsmouth
Poulton-le-Fylde
Preston
Prestwich
Pudsey
Radcliffe
RAF Chivenor
RAF Cosford
RAF Hawkinge
RAF Manston
RAF Manston: A Second Selection
RAF St Mawgan
RAF Tangmere
Ramsgate & Thanet Life
Reading
Reading: A Second Selection
Redditch & the Needle District
Redditch: A Second Selection
Richmond, Surrey
Rickmansworth
Around Ripley
The River Soar
Romney Marsh
Romney Marsh: A Second Selection
Rossendale
Around Rotherham
Rugby
Around Rugeley
Ruislip
Around Ryde
St Albans
St Andrews
Salford
Salisbury
Salisbury: A Second Selection
Salisbury: A Third Selection
Around Salisbury
Sandhurst & Crowthorne
Sandown & Shanklin
Sandwich
Scarborough
Scunthorpe
Seaton, Lyme Regis & Axminster
Around Seaton & Sidmouth
Sedgley & District
The Severn Vale
Sherwood Forest
Shrewsbury
Shrewsbury: A Second Selection
Shropshire Railways
Skegness
Around Skegness
Skipton & the Dales
Around Slough
Smethwick
Somerton & Langport
Southampton
Southend-on-Sea
Southport
Southwark
Southwell
Southwold to Aldeburgh
Stafford
Around Stafford
Staffordshire Railways
Around Staveley
Stepney
Stevenage
The History of Stilton Cheese
Stoke-on-Trent
Stoke Newington
Stonehouse to Painswick
Around Stony Stratford
Around Stony Stratford: A Second Selection
Stowmarket
Streatham
Stroud & the Five Valleys
Stroud & the Five Valleys: A Second Selection
Stroud's Golden Valley
The Stroudwater and Thames & Severn Canals
The Stroudwater and Thames & Severn Canals: A Second Selection
Suffolk at Work
Suffolk at Work: A Second Selection
The Heart of Suffolk
Sunderland
Sutton
Swansea
Swindon: A Third Selection
Swindon: A Fifth Selection
Around Tamworth
Taunton
Around Taunton
Teesdale
Teesdale: A Second Selection
Tenbury Wells
Around Tettenhall & Codshall
Tewkesbury & the Vale of Gloucester
Thame to Watlington
Around Thatcham
Around Thirsk
Thornbury to Berkeley
Tipton
Around Tonbridge
Trowbridge
Around Truro
TT Races
Tunbridge Wells
Tunbridge Wells: A Second Selection
Twickenham
Uley, Dursley & Cam
The Upper Fal
The Upper Tywi Valley
Uxbridge, Hillingdon & Cowley
The Vale of Belvoir
The Vale of Conway
Ventnor
Wakefield
Wallingford
Walsall
Waltham Abbey
Wandsworth at War
Wantage, Faringdon & the Vale Villages
Around Warwick
Weardale
Weardale: A Second Selection
Wednesbury
Wells
Welshpool
West Bromwich
West Wight
Weston-super-Mare
Around Weston-super-Mare
Weymouth & Portland
Around Wheatley
Around Whetstone
Whitchurch to Market Drayton
Around Whitstable
Wigton & the Solway Plain
Willesden
Around Wilton
Wimbledon
Around Windsor
Wingham, Addisham & Littlebourne
Wisbech
Witham & District
Witney
Around Witney
The Witney District
Wokingham
Around Woodbridge
Around Woodstock
Woolwich
Woolwich Royal Arsenal
Around Wootton Bassett, Cricklade & Purton
Worcester
Worcester in a Day
Around Worcester
Worcestershire at Work
Around Worthing
Wotton-under-Edge to Chipping Sodbury
Wymondham & Attleborough
The Yorkshire Wolds